LIVING LIFE WITH PURPOSE

SHARON BOTTS GARTH

authorHOUSE®

AuthorHouse™
1663 Liberty Drive
Bloomington, IN 47403
www.authorhouse.com
Phone: 1 (800) 839-8640

Published by AuthorHouse 05/29/2019

ISBN: 978-1-5462-6013-4 (sc)
ISBN: 978-1-5462-6011-0 (hc)
ISBN: 978-1-5462-6012-7 (e)

Library of Congress Control Number: 2018910988

Rev. Henry W Botts Sr.

Author
Sharon Botts Garth

Contents

Contents

Preface

As the author, I'm telling Rev. Henry W. Botts Sr., my grandfather's story because he was an amazing man who related to everyone regardless of race, age or culture. He used his wisdom, traits of abiding love and compassion to reach, teach and empower generations. His goal was to create environments where everyone could pursue their hopes, dreams and live together in harmony.

He focused on shaping individuals and families to love, respect and show accountability for one another. He knew, how you treat someone is who they will become. He taught love because it anchors our character, beliefs, and values. Next, he focused on respect to ensure the relational boundaries were held in high regard ensuring that every station in life was autonomous, recognized, understood, and celebrated. Finally, he applied accountability for one another as a principle to unify and strengthen the individual, family and community bond.

Early in life, he realized his purpose; the reason he was in the world, was to teach others how to embrace and care for humanity and the earth. He used his life to demonstrate how to live victoriously and make a difference in the lives of others. As a minister, he impacted people's lives by leading them to Christ and ensuring their soul's salvation.

As I follow in his footsteps, I plan to use the tools and resources he has given to continue his ministry of teaching, inspiring and empowering generations. His ministry helped to build character which enhanced purpose and created successful outcomes.

Chapter 1

SEEKING LIFE'S PURPOSE

My name is Sharon Botts Garth. I am the granddaughter of the late Reverend Henry W. Botts Sr., who lived an amazing life full of dignity and purpose.

I'm telling his story to demonstrate that every person has the power of God within them to positively impact the world around them. His life teaches us to know and walk in your purpose. It is the cornerstone of living life victoriously. Whether modest or gregarious, rich or poor, I want future generations to know the power to achieve and positively impact social and political environments. When you live your purpose as shown by this ordinary man, you will be blessed to conquer life situations.

Grandfather was born in 1875, 10 years after the abolishment of slavery. He and his siblings were the first generation of black Botts to be born free on plantation land. He was a very proud, yet introspective, man who cared deeply about the conditions forced upon his race. Grandfather was small in stature, 5'8" and 140 pounds. His head was always held high and he spoke with authority, but his voice was soft and soothing. He was a self-taught man. His formal schooling ended after the eighth grade. He was forced to work in the fields to help support the family.

He was known to say, "I live in two worlds, here and beyond," because he spent a great deal of time in meditation and preparation. The time he spent in meditation and prayer prepared him to become completely dependent on the Lord; only following what God would have him do. He knew the best way to become an effective leader was to show people how to live, survive and prosper.

I believe he was preordained to lead, protect, and nurture the people with whom he came in contact. He was born to complete the assignment for the purpose of glorifying God. His obedience to God was rewarded at every juncture of his life. God fulfilled the promise written in the bible by blessing him, his ministry and the people he served.

Through the teachings of Rev. Botts, the people grew closer to God and their lives were enhanced. They worked together to glorify God and the families prospered. Because of their steadfast love, each church along Rev. Botts journey grew and has stood the test of time. Each church becoming beacons in the night showing the light illuminated by Jesus Christ.

He nurtured and loved his family, congregations, and communities; and in return they loved him. Grandfathers life is a model for church leaders of today. The model encourages them to embrace and teach future generations to succeed.

Gentry Street Baptist Church
2010

I decided to trace my roots following the passing of my father, Rev. Henry W. Botts Jr. My husband Rev. Gerald Garth and I decided to take a road trip to find what information remained about the black Botts. We arranged to meet a cousin Mary Ann Botts Dunlap and her mother Martha Darlene Botts when we arrived. I was curious to learn if there would be any trace of black existence in the small rural southern town of Meadville Missouri. Meadville is a small town approximately 60 miles south of the Iowa border with a population of 450 people. There was no visible industry, only single-family houses. The town was known as a bedroom community; a place where people live after working in another town.

When we spoke to the grocer at the general store he said, black Botts' no longer lived in Meadville. He directed us down the street to the corner of Gentry and Main. He told us we would find the black church there and around the corner, there would be a cemetery where both black and white Botts were buried.

As we stood in front of the old dilapidated wood-frame building, I could see it had been vandalized and almost destroyed. The name affixed to the front of the building identified the structure as Gentry Street Baptist Church. Most of the paint had chipped away and the wood frame was slanting slightly to the left as if it could not stand much longer. As we went inside, the wooden floor had obvious gaps, dips and what remained had been severely damaged by the rain. I looked up and saw a large hole where the church bell when rung, sang out welcoming notes inviting parishioners to Sunday Service. The bell had rung for over 100 years and was now silenced.

As we walked further into the chapel, we could see the pews, piano, and the pulpit had been removed. We were all saddened to see the condition of the building and the lack of concern for its contents. But somehow, as I stood there, I felt a kinship to that old building, because it was sold to members of the black Botts family as a place of worship, in 1889.

I now also felt a strong sense of pride as I walked through the rundown structure. I thought to myself, this could be one of the last remaining structures in this country to hold the stories of the lives and struggles of Southern blacks before and after the abolishment of slavery in 1865. It could be the final remnant representing the family roots of many black families who contributed greatly to the success of the community and left their legacy in the sands of time, including mine. At that moment, the old church became a symbol of adversity, struggle, pain, and the rewards that many black community members had experienced. It symbolized the resilience of those who survived.

As we drove, we came upon a cemetery originally called Botts Cemetery. As we walked the grounds, I was able to identify many of the black ancestors based upon the information that my grandfather had shared with me. It was wonderful to see the final resting place where white and blacks were buried together. This was an indication of how the white and black families had grown to respect, care, and work together to create a vital community.

My grandfather was a product of this community, and he lived his life with purpose, dignity, and grace. He followed the examples of being God-fearing, loving, and steadfast, which he learned from his community. Those characteristics put him on a path where he was one with his purpose. He was always focused on the future, not troubled by the past and was he was intent on reaching his goal. He was known for saying, "I'd rather see a sermon lived than to preach one," which is how he lived his life.

Initially, grandfather's parents were slaves brought to farm the land. Their earliest existence can be traced back to the 1840 census when they were living on the land. Following the abolishment of slavery and the enactment of the Homestead Act of 1866, many of the Botts families agreed to purchase land. They lived on the land, earning income from the sale of crops to repay the debt. They used the remaining money to take care of their families. The parcels of land were divided among the families who chose to stay and take advantage of ownership.

From early in his childhood he knew not to speak unless spoken to especially in the presence of white folks. He also knew to do what he was told without question and to never look a white person in the eye because he was not their equal. It was necessary to always show a subservient posture. An accusation from a white person, true or false, was cause for punishment, such as being hung, castrated or dismembered; or in rare cases when imprisoned, be sentenced to death.

Even though grandfather witnessed those incidents, he learned not to allow fear, blame, shame, jealousy or anger to control him. He had seen how those emotions destroyed an individual's ability to think rationally, remain calm, and centered. To keep the black children of the community safe, their parents negotiated a process with white leaders of the community where their children would not be punished or harmed if they followed the rules.

The first bible verses that were taught to the children was *Mark. 12:30 and thou shall love the Lord thy God with all thy heart, and with all thy soul, and with all thy mind, and with all thy strength* and verse *31, the second is this, thou shall love thy neighbor as thyself. There is no other commandment greater than these.*

Children often went to neighboring communities to distribute eggs and crops or pick up needed supplies for the family. The parents used those verses as codes to teach them what to say if questioned by a white person outside the community. This teaching provided the children who could not roam freely, outside of the black community an explanation of how to respond.

If a black person was seen outside the community and a white person questioned them as to where they were going and why; the children were to use the first code of giving their family name and the name of the landowner. The second code instructed the children to always pray to the Heavenly Father when being questioned about their destination. They were taught to believe you are under Gods protection and only the holy spirit can touch the heart of the accuser or questioner and have them do the right thing, mainly let the children proceed on their journey. Only blacks who were an acceptable member of the overall community could use this process. If you were not a member of the community, you could be detained and severely punished.

Grandfathers determination to remain safe and free kept him on the path of building a loving spiritual relationship with God. He was always mindful of how he sought God in the little one-room building called Gentry Street Baptist Church around 1883. He remained steadfast in his beliefs and unconstrained as he continued along life's journey.

The stories he shared with me were about his life, the names of the family members, and their relationships. I wrote down all the information he gave to me and kept it in a secret place, so I'd always be able to find it when needed. The year grandfather's stories began was 1955 and I was about 9 years old. Grandfather was the fifth child born to Thomas and Matilda Botts.

Great-grandfather Thomas and great-grandmother Matilda were brought to Meadville to care for the family of John Botts. Their names along with their six children Thomas, Virginia, Margaret, William, Henry, and Elizabeth can be found in the 1850 census data.

Large parcels of land were sold to the former slaves of the Botts family signaling the abolishment of slavery, and grandfather Henry's parents were now sharecroppers. The indebtedness would be repaid through the annual sale of crops. The former slaves felt they could farm, live on the land and become contributing members of the community. They learned that paying off the debt was harder than it looked on paper. Most sharecroppers ended up owing one-third to one-half of the sale of their crops annually to pay off their debt. They started to question how they were to take care of their families during the year if much of their annual earnings was slated to pay for the land.

They were able to make a living and supporting their families, by raising chickens, cattle and harvesting large gardens of fruits and vegetables all of which provided income for the family. They worked from sunup to sundown and every family member had responsibilities to fulfill. Young Henry and his older brother William were two of the younger children, who fed the chickens, fetched the water and worked in the garden.

The families learned to work together. One or two families would buy the food necessary to sustain them for the first quarter of the year. The next quarter another group of families would take over that same responsibility. Several of the families were responsible for mending tattered clothing. The remaining families in the community would take charge of seeking, securing, then storing the heating oil and getting the wood for the stoves. That way no family had to use all their resources. The men hunted, the women cooked, baked and washed clothes.

The former slaves took on the surname Botts from the original land-owner to symbolize their heritage and the opportunity to live good lives debt free on the land. They were resilient and resourceful, and it paid off. Later, they were able to acquire a school-house to educate their children.

Grandfathers humble beginnings taught him to have a strong work ethic and perseverance. He also learned to treat people with respect, which served him well when he grew old enough to sell crops at the families outside the market. Many of grandfather's patrons were from the white community and they seemed to get a lot of enjoyment from his persistence when selling crops and other products. He could tell them why they needed certain fruits and vegetables; or, other handmade products made by black women. As a young lad, grandfather became quite a conversationalist and, in his words, "people would buy stuff from me just so I'd stop talking so much." Then he'd give a shrill laugh and his eyes would twinkle.

Grandfather was very ambitious and developed his preaching skills at a young age. In his spare time, he would hold church and would act out each of the roles by praying, singing and preaching to the glory of God. It didn't matter to him whether others came to listen or not. He was on a mission and he diligently prepared himself for the journey that was to come.

He talked about how his modest beginnings also taught him to look for every opportunity to make a living. Sharecropping was hard work and he knew it was not his passion. Instead, he received great pleasure in talking to people, finding out who they were, and how to meet their needs. He prided himself in being an observant communicator which made him a great salesman and future leader!

Early on he dedicated his life to the betterment of people, and he found his platform and his voice in service to the community through the church. He studied the Bible late at night after everyone was asleep. It was during this time that he found a scripture that would guide and direct his focus for the rest of his life. Psalms 73:24, *"You guide me with your counsel leading me to a glorious destiny,"* this became the foundation for his life's work, and he chose to follow the teachings of God. This scripture set him on the path to developing a steadfast relationship with God the Father. Through that relationship he began to align his character with the purpose for which he was created and, he followed in the footsteps of Jesus which he knew would lead him to successfully accomplish his goals.

He did not want his parents to know his desire to leave the farm and pursue a calling to go into the ministry. There was no money for him to go to college, so he read the Bible and all the books on Biblical teaching and preaching that he could get from preachers in the ministry. He watched and followed the ministers closely and finally caught the eye of a minister who agreed to mentor him and formally prepare him for the ministry.

The way he lived his life is a demonstration of how he took what he learned and used it to teach others. He used his experiences to build strong families that supported the needs of the communities he served throughout his lifetime. He used his voice to reveal God's grace and mercy by leading families and communities to work together, supporting and trusting each other for the greater good of the community. He became a community organizer, change agent, and a revered Christian leader.

When in his twenties, grandfather married a lady our family only knew as Bottsie. Initially, he was a traveling pastor who performed church services in several of the rural communities in Missouri. His wife and small child Gladys usually did not travel with him. Bottsie kept the home and cared for the child. When Bottsie became ill, her family came and took her and her daughter home with them to another county to nurse her back to health. No one living in Meadville can recall why Bottsie and Gladys did not return to the small community, but they were never seen in Meadville again.

In his thirties, grandfather married Sarah Jane Henderson and they had three children: Carmen Marsel (1904), Henry Wilson Jr. (1907), and Ella Naomi (1911). An older woman, a midwife whose name was Mrs. Holiday, became Sarah's best friend. A few years after Ella's birth, around 1915, Sarah contracted influenza. Mrs. Holiday took care of Sarah and the children, but as fate would have it, Sarah passed away; leaving grandfather to raise three small children alone. Mrs. Holiday agreed to stay on with grandfather to raise and nurture the children.

Chapter 2

A TIME OF TRANSITION

The first time that destiny called, grandfather was chosen to pastor Second Baptist Church in Plattsburg, MO. This arrangement was very important to his future because he could keep his family together and continue to pursue his ministerial work. Prayer was an ongoing part of grandfather's daily routine and before he made any life-changing decisions, he would take the situation to the Lord for direction and guidance.

In order to accomplish his goal of becoming a Senior Pastor of a larger church and having a positive impact on the lives of men and women, he knew he needed to be in the will of God. Only through God could he provide comfort and compassion to those who struggled to maintain their families and provide a meaningful future for their children. When he received the confirmation from God to move forward and take the position, he was thrilled to be taking on the responsibilities of Senior Pastor and having the opportunity to nurture and grow a church.

He was always an avid reader but now he could devote even more time to learning and meditation. His determination to make life better for the people he shepherded led him to create a step by step mentoring program. It was called "Success Now," to teach his parishioners self-sufficiency. The program he developed taught people to work in small groups, divide up responsibilities and give each person an opportunity to perform each role. Everyone learned the responsibility of both leading and following in a group setting. This program created a very tight-knit community where members could rely on each other to accomplish their goals.

Soon after he took on more responsibilities with the National Baptist Convention. He became known as an eloquent speaker and Bible teacher. Working in the National Baptist Convention gave him the visibility and opportunity to become well known throughout the region. He traveled extensively and created a very successful ministry in Plattsburg MO. He ministered at Second Baptist Church for 8 years and his name is displayed on the cornerstone of the Church. He was known as the Pastor responsible for creating the building fund which was used to enhance most of today's current church structure. He also pastored a church in Boonville MO for a couple of years before he accepted the next pastoral position.

Second Baptist Church
Plattsburg MO – 2010

Rev. Botts next calling was to become the Senior Pastor at Lincoln, Nebraska's Mount Zion Baptist Church. Rev. Botts, being an eloquent preacher and a charismatic man of God, soon became a spokesman regarding the issues facing the Black Community. Social, political and civic community meetings were held at Mount Zion because the facility could accommodate larger groups.

In the dedication booklet of Mount Zion Baptist Church, dated September 30, 1973, Rev. Botts ministry was described as follows: Rev. H. W. Botts began his role as pastor the second Sunday in October 1920. He was the most energetic pastor ever called by the church in planning for its general welfare. He led the planning meetings for the rebuilding of the church which was approved and began in 1922. The rebuilding project also included the addition of an auditorium which was completed in 1924. Many families with children joined the church under his leadership because he had the ability to engage them in church ministry services; food shelves, clothing, transportation, health care, and day-care. Being involved in these ministry services not only lifted them up from despair and poverty but taught them to support others.

Grandfather was the community representative and spokesperson who was on call for every community service and event. The Negro newspaper, the Lincoln Gazette, covered all the black community news on a weekly basis. Most events were held at Zion where Rev. Botts and members of the church leadership group always participated.

Mount Zion Baptist Church

Lincoln Nebraska – 1920's

Shortly after Rev. Botts moved to Lincoln to accept a pastoral position, his older brother Rev. William Fred Botts was called to pastor the largest Baptist church in Omaha, Nebraska called Zion Baptist Church. Rev. Botts's name is etched on the cornerstone of that church which still stands. Following his tenure in Omaha, he accepted a call to a church in California where he pastored until his death.

In 1925 and again in 1929 destiny called Rev. Botts to be considered as pastor in Minneapolis, Minnesota at Zion Baptist Church. The search committee was seeking a Senior Pastor in 1925 and they contacted Rev. Lee Ware Harris of Pilgrim Baptist Church in Saint Paul, Minnesota to ask for recommendations. Because of the strong connection between Pilgrim Baptist Church and Zion Baptist Church, Rev. Harris recommended Rev. Henry W. Botts, Sr., for the position. He already had the successful pastoral experience they needed to positively impact church growth and strengthen communities for the future.

During Rev. Botts first visit to Zion, he laid out his goals and objectives to move the church forward. He established the framework for preparing black families who would come "Up North" in search of new opportunities to work. He stressed the need to seek black leaders from the South to prepare the southerners for the cultural changes they would experience. He was not selected for the position because he was unmarried. The church thought it could be controversial to have an unmarried minister in charge of a congregation whose makeup was predominately widowers and single women.

Rev. Botts continued to minister at Mount Zion in Lincoln and soon met and married Ursula Hines from St. Joseph, Missouri, in 1927. Mrs. Holiday, the midwife who cared for the family during the last decade, decided to return to her home in Missouri. Losing Mrs. Holiday proved to be problematic for the children. They regarded her leaving as another loss in their lives. Although the older two children were young adults, they resented losing Mrs. Holiday and drifted away from the family with plans to start their own lives.

In 1928 Zion Baptist Church in Minneapolis was without a pastor again and they revisited the idea of Rev. Botts being considered for the position especially now that he had a wife and fully met all the requirements. My grandmother, Mrs. Ursula Hines Botts, was a spiritual woman; a helpmate and a leader in the women's movement dating back to the early 1920s before she met and married grandfather.

Mrs. Botts, a leader in the Ancient Egyptian Arabic Order of Noble Mystic Shrine, held the office of Imperial Commandress from 1923-1925. The Ancient Egyptian Arabic Order is the philanthropic arm of the Shrine through which a college scholarship was named after Mrs. Botts. The scholarship is still in existence today, and 90 years since its inception, is still used as a source of financial assistance for young women who are seeking college degrees. Grandmother was always active in the order of the Eastern Star and rose to the position of Worthy Grand Matron of the

National Organization which was the highest level of leadership in the organization. She held the highest level of leadership. The relationship between Rev. and Mrs. Botts was a love affair that lasted over 50 years until he passed at the age of 92.

Mrs. Ursula Hines Botts
Imperial Commandress

Grandfather and grandmother held a meeting to let the children Carmen, Henry Jr. and Ella know that he was offered the position as Senior Pastor at a church "Up North." They would be moving to Minnesota to take on the responsibilities of a new church. They asked their children whether they wanted to join them in the move to Minnesota and felt the move might benefit them because blacks had a better chance of securing work and having a stable future.

The younger Botts had other ideas. Carmen and Ella now living in Kansas City, Missouri decided to stay where they were because they were making a living and supporting themselves and Ella's 2 girls; Faye and Carol. Henry Jr. was planning to pursue a music career in Chicago Illinois, so he moved to Milwaukee Wisconsin for a couple of years to earn additional income before venturing on to Chicago and entering the entertainment field. Grandfather and grandmother readied themselves to move and continue to pursue their personal life goals of serving others and making communities strong.

The call to fulfill destiny was different this time. Rev. Botts accepted the position, and let his wife and family know this move would be his last. He felt that God was assigning him to a glorious place where he would live out the rest of his life serving God and leading people. Later in life, my grandmother would corroborate my grandfather's stories and she said, he told her with confidence that we will not move anymore. This will be our home until the end.

Even though making a major life change was difficult, they were also very happy and grateful for the opportunity to have a new beginning. Grandfather arrived in Minneapolis with his wife Ursula, just a few months before the Stock Market Crash of 1929. Rev. Henry W. Botts Sr., went on to become one of Minnesota's most influential and highly regarded black leaders.

Zion Baptist Church
1023 Lyndale Avenue North

When grandfather arrived in Minneapolis, the first contact he made was to his lifelong friend Rev. Lee Ware Harris. Rev. Botts and Rev. Harris grew up in neighboring Missouri communities close to Boone County where the famed Rev. Robert Hickman, and 75 other slaves, made the voyage up the Mississippi River to freedom in Minnesota. Hickman stood against compromising their beliefs or religious practices and fought for religious freedom to worship God in their own way. They loudly and mournfully expressed their thankfulness to God for his grace and mercy which saved them, protected them, and often led them out of harm's way on their journey "Up North."

Rev. Hickman is credited with being responsible for the initial migration of black people from Missouri to Minnesota. They founded several black churches; Pilgrim Baptist Church in St. Paul, Zion Baptist Church in North Minneapolis, St. James AME Church in South Minneapolis, and a church in Duluth.

There were many other stories they shared with the church parishioners. They talked about their early lives growing up in Missouri. Their parents' stories about slavery and how Missouri became a Midwest state where one could pass over into freedom. Once slaves reached the middle passage, they were told to find the pathways which led to the border. The middle part of the country was occupied by the Native Americans who would be forced to move farther west to accommodate the Government's plan to extend its territory. The new territory would be sold to the settlers to inhabit and create new communities. Eastern settlers moved west to occupy land now known as Missouri.

Rev. Henry and Ursula Botts, Sr.
Zion Baptist Church

Many of Missouri's counties had large numbers of slaves who were bought by new settlers to cultivate the land. Several of the counties were in central Missouri. The Missouri River ran through the middle passage, as it made its way to join the Mississippi River on the eastern side of Missouri. It provided the needed shelter and sources of food for runaway slaves. This area was less than 60 miles from the border of Iowa which meant freedom to those slaves who were fleeing the oppression of the south.

Runaway slaves knew if they could get to the middle passage in Missouri, there was a plan to help them get to freedom. The Native Americans and slaves used their knowledge of the terrain, and black churches like Gentry Street Baptist to develop safe places for runaway slaves to stop along the way. The Native Americans also built special tree shelters where fleeing slaves could hide and go unnoticed as they made their way to the border.

As oral tradition would have it, the two younger pastors learned their history from their forefathers by word of mouth. This was the way they ensured that the younger generations knew the danger of being black and living in a racially motivated society. It was imperative that the younger generations knew their worth. Until the abolishment of slavery, blacks were classified as property in the census data. The designation of being classified as 3/5 a man made them dispensable with no rights under the constitution. Having this knowledge kept young blacks from quibbling with whites over things they could not control.

When the travelers reached the shores of St. Paul Minnesota, they were notified of the government plan to disperse them across the state preventing a heavy concentration of blacks taking local jobs from white laborers. The plan was to send some of the travelers to Duluth, some to North Minneapolis, some to South Minneapolis and the remainder would stay in St. Paul.

The story-tellers emphasized the fact that attitudes of Northern whites were not very different than the attitudes of Southern whites. The difference between the North and the South were their laws. Slavery was not practiced in the North nor were the Jim Crow or Black Code laws which made being black a punishable crime for any infraction. The North was segregated, and blacks were not treated equally. The acceptance of segregation; regardless of geography, made it safer and more economically feasible for blacks to live together, look out for each other and share resources. The use of that model produced the greatest success the black communities of America have known.

Only 30 miles and 20 years separated Rev. Hickman's voyage up the Mississippi and the birth of the two pastors. The power of the two pastors passing on the stories has kept the history and legacy of slaves successfully reaching freedom for generations. Rev. Botts and Rev. Harris remained close friends and worked together on matters facing the black community in the Twin Cities and the National Baptist Convention during their years together in Minnesota. As the years progressed, they were also very influential in attracting fellow Missourians and other Southerners to move to Minnesota to experience an environment where injustices could be confronted. There was also a growing economic forecast and the outlook was more favorable for black folks "Up North."

Chapter 3

BEGINNING THE JOURNEY
OF FULFILLMENT

The Botts thought of the move as a new beginning with the possibility of new opportunities to prosper in a Northern state. When the Botts arrived in Minnesota, they were entering a new frontier and were pioneers in a sense. Bravely moving to a community they did not know to care for and serve families they had yet to meet. Instead, they were received like royalty. The congregation and the community welcomed them with open arms, and they were accepted.

Grandfather always commented; "being assigned to Zion Baptist Church in Minneapolis became his third appointment to a church named Zion." This appointment was very significant to him. In the Bible, Zion represents both a city of David and the city of God." To grandfather, this symbolized that God had chosen him to accomplish extraordinary work. Then with his bold sense of humor, he'd laugh and say, "either God loves me very much or he needs to keep me very close to him." He chose to believe that both statements were true, and he was blessed!

Even though Minneapolis was a Northern city it was still very much segregated and there were plenty of challenges for black families to overcome. Succeeding through this part of the journey required an abiding love of Jesus Christ and the desire to do the will of God.

As soon as the Botts arrived in Minneapolis, they went to work implementing grandfather's plan to create stability and growth within the church. His plan was very strategic; originating from his years of experiences as a young lad growing up in a very segregated Southern community. He met with the leaders of the church to lay out his plan to prepare parishioners to imitate the love of Jesus Christ and to build strong relationships to attract and retain new members. As he prepared the leaders, he taught them to dedicate their lives to living as God would have them live. Then he forged ahead, reaching and saving more and more souls to join the house of God.

Zion Baptist Church Children's Baptism

The American Industrialization intensified during the 1930s and '40s as people moved North and West. Many jobs were consolidated into industry groups such as; railroads, financial, telecommunications, technology, etc. Many of the jobs created by the new industries required additional skills. The new jobs afforded black people the opportunity to get a job, work 9 to 5 and receive a weekly or monthly paycheck for their work. This way of life became attractive to many southern blacks who were still sharecropping to make a living. Working sunup to sundown and rarely making enough to survive was reason enough for Southern blacks to consider moving North. They chose cities where new jobs were being created and they could take advantage of making a living to provide better lives for their families.

Now a self-made leader, Rev. Botts taught himself to preach and teach from the Bible at a very early age. He attracted new families who left their homes and familiar surroundings, in search of a better future. His stories brought them into the church because his life experiences were very similar. Rev. Botts messages were not intended to stir up negative emotions, but to teach how God could bring them through situations if they trusted and had faith. He taught the people to become self-reliant by working, living in unity and depending on their strength and purpose. He lived the example he taught others to follow.

By 1930 Rev. and Mrs. Botts were an integral part of life in Minneapolis and Zion Baptist Church. Families lived in North Minneapolis, South Minneapolis or Saint Paul and most held jobs such as railroad porters, domestic and postal workers, and some were fortunate enough to own their own businesses. The Twin Cities was a close-knit community where relatives and friends from the various communities gathered on the weekends and holidays to stay connected. Many of them followed the teaching of Rev. Botts to use their money wisely by saving, investing, purchasing homes and owning businesses. They created their own personal wealth and became self-sufficient.

He also taught the importance of having the proper insurances to ensure the family could survive even thrive if something happened to the major breadwinner. Owning your own business provided pathways into industries which did not hire blacks like; insurance. If, you started an insurance business and sold policies the major companies would want to partner with you or buy you out. This became another way of securing a future for their family. It was very important to him that everyone learned to take care of their personal affairs. Grandfather was known as a community builder because of his teachings on self-preservation and internal community reliance. He was always teaching the power of independence and self-sufficiency which made the people and community strong and prosperous.

Downtown was segregated and there were very few stores where blacks could shop. Many bathrooms were closed to black shoppers, not by a sign on the door but a locked door where you had to seek an employee to get the key, but if you were black, the key was never available. Blacks could not eat at the lunch counters, not because of a sign on the wall, but because no one would serve them. These are only a couple of examples of the discrimination they faced.

Zion Baptist Church's previous location was on Border Street in North Minneapolis before the Great Depression. There was a fire in the church which destroyed the entire upstairs and required them to hold service in the basement. The church leadership along with Rev. Botts started looking for a new facility. They contacted the Twin Cities Baptist Union for financial support. The union agreed to purchase the building at 1023 Lyndale Avenue North, a former Jewish Synagogue for $7,000.00. It was difficult for blacks to get loans; particularly to purchase a building; however, the Baptist Union having faith in Rev. Botts felt he could run a smooth operation, and willingly loaned the amount needed. Their hunch paid off when Zion Baptist Church retired the mortgage ahead of schedule! That was a glorious time of celebration and thanksgiving.

A few years later, Zion also purchased the parsonage at 1019 Lyndale Avenue North. The intersection where Zion was located was home to several historic businesses. Theodore Woodard, a close friend of Rev. Botts, owned Woodard's Funeral Chapel on one corner. A Fire Department and a bar called the "Blue Note" were located on the other two corners making the intersection one of the most controversial corners in North Minneapolis. The differing cultures and lifestyles of each establishment created conflicts from time to time. Then it would become necessary for the organizational leaders to intervene to find solutions and resolve the situation.

Rev. Botts often told the congregation, "Zion is the church where everyone is somebody and we're all equal in the sight of God." His message was so important to people who were looking for hope and needed to be recognized as equals; especially, in the house of God. He set the tone for how his parishioners were to treat one another by teaching them to look for daily opportunities to help someone.

One example he used was to keep tokens which could be given to someone who needed to catch the streetcar.

Another example was to keep extra change available for people who were short on the grocery bill at the store. It was in his nature to care about people who were less fortunate and to encourage others to do the same. This method of caring for one another was an important part of how he kept the morale up in the community by not focusing on what they did not have; but instead, what they could do for each other.

Blacks who were contributing members of society could still face racial bias at work, while shopping, or riding the streetcar. That was the reason the church was the place outside the home where everyone was somebody. When they entered the doors of the church, they needed to find hope, kindness and a helping hand. Everyone was treated fairly in the church and Rev. Botts taught them to teach each other the skills and knowledge necessary to survive and make good decisions. Families of doctors, lawyers and architects sat next to domestic and sanitation workers in the church. Doctors, lawyers, and architects attended the weekly or monthly training programs bringing with them the skills and knowledge that laborers, and domestic workers would not be privy to in their jobs.

They became resources for each other and when a family was in need, regardless of status, the whole church rallied around them to meet their needs. Moving to Minneapolis and other communities "Up North" was a step up for many black families, who no longer had to toil from sun up to sun down in the fields. They no longer had to work day after day picking cotton for pennies or being treated as less than human.

Minneapolis was basically a rural community, many of the streets were still unpaved and many roads were traveled by horse and buggy. It was also a growing metropolis which offered the potential for better jobs, education, and housing. Neighborhood children, regardless of color, attended John Hay Elementary, Lincoln or Franklin Junior High School. After leaving Jr. High, most northside children entered North High School or the Vocational School downtown. They played sports at Sumner Field, studied at Sumner

Library, and attended social events at Phyliss Wheatley Settlement House. Most of the families in North Minneapolis were black, white or Jewish and lived harmoniously on the same side of town. Although most blacks lived in substandard housing in small segregated sections of North Minneapolis; the rent was more affordable.

The black community experienced many struggles during the economic downturns of the 1920s and '30s. Sometimes they struggled to feed and clothe their children. Many were consumed with making sure their children received a good education and were properly prepared for the future. They wanted to ensure that future generations would have the opportunity to succeed and prosper.

In the '30s and 40's most of the property which housed black families had wood cooking and heating stoves with no running water or electricity. Seeing chickens, eggs and small farm animals in the backyards of North Minneapolis houses was not unusual. Weekly, the deliverymen brought ice, milk, bread, wood, and coal.

The saying in the black community was "anyone who wants to work can find a job in Minneapolis." Black people did find work and were eventually able to improve the living standards of their families. They moved across Olson Highway to houses previously occupied by the Jewish community where more substantial housing was becoming available.

The black population was estimated to be less than 1% of the total population. With such a small black population everyone in the community knew each other. Even though there were several black churches in the Twin Cities, everyone knew the other churchgoers because they were related or they lived in the same neighborhoods; so, they worshiped and socialized together frequently.

Zion Baptist Church Sunday School
1930's

Zion's congregation reached approximately 250 members during the 1930s. The young people would say, "if your family lives in Minneapolis, Rev. Botts either christened, baptized, married or buried someone in your family." The church was the hub of black existence and pride. It was the place which met many of the needs of the black community. Whether you were homeless, without food, lost your job, had an emergency expense or lost a loved one; the church was the place where you could receive the assistance and support you needed. No matter where you came from, no matter your circumstances you were welcomed and embraced at Zion.

Cecil Newman was the Editor of the Minneapolis Spokesman and the Saint Paul Recorder. The papers covered the community news such as; political, civic and social events to keep the black community informed about stories of interest and importance. Included in the papers was a section called "Church News" which covered the highlights of Twin Cities church's weekly activities. Zion Baptist Church and many other churches were featured weekly for the time Rev. Botts pastored at Zion. Cecil Newman and Rev. Botts were colleagues and they supported many civic, political and social events which focused on enlightening and uplifting the black community.

Families, particularly families from Missouri, where my grandfather grew up and began his ministry, flocked to Minneapolis because they heard of the wonderful ministerial work that Rev. Botts was providing. The stories went out that he was changing the lives of black people by being engaged with the NAACP, the Urban League and the Unions. He and others assembled groups of people to address the negative impact of segregation on the advancement of the community of black folks. Whether the issue was substandard housing, poor public-school education or unfair labor practices and low wages he was there. He was addressing and challenging the status quo.

Grandfather's involvement in significant community issues grew as the community grew. He coached and assisted people from the community in a unique manner. He assumed the role of advocate often speaking on their behalf even when he barely knew them. He was acutely aware of the circumstances under which they were being judged and he understood the potential outcome.

He was a very skilled negotiator who would fight to resolve situations in a manner that would keep the person whole, when possible. He often used the example of the golden rule, "do unto others as you would have them do unto you," or "love thy neighbor as thyself," as the foundation for his appeal. He put together so many appeals using those two phrases, you would figure the lawyers and judges would have found a repeal for his arguments. But instead, they seemed to be defenseless against him. Everyone that Rev. Botts spoke in defense of was treated fairly by the courts and the judges.

Being a pastor and one who turned so many lives around, he gained a strong reputation for fairness and the ability to neutralize and resolve issues. He often arranged for a person to work off the debt if something was stolen or needed to be replaced, rather than going to jail for a small infraction. His intention was to keep people as contributing members of society and not allow the stereotypes of fear and prejudice to prevail and take away a person's freedom.

Minnesota Governor's Elmer Anderson and Karl Rolvaag's offices often contacted grandfather to attend meetings of community importance. Whether there was a killing across racial lines, wage disputes between companies and workers, unreasonable or unfair court decisions against a community member, Rev. Botts was called to assist in calming the situation and finding an amicable solution.

Chapter 4

A FAITH WALK

The Great Migration from the South to the North began during the 1920s and intensified during the '30s and '40s. There was a huge change in the demographics as more and more blacks moved to northern cities including Minneapolis. The great migration took place when the laws governing slavery were repealed but replaced by new laws such as the Black Code and Jim Crow. These new laws created the loss of jobs, poor wages, and unsafe living conditions. It became more dangerous for blacks to live in the South with the enforcement of the Black Code which took away the components of freedom; like ownership, self-employment or the inability to prove that you worked for a white person.

The enforcement of Jim Crow laws perpetuated racial segregation. Ideologies of separating the two races allowed white government and business leaders to funnel the resources into the white community. The black community was left without resources or support to grow or develop and black people were treated as less than a white person with no rights or methods of recourse.

This law made blacks the target of racism and violence. Black people could be hung or sentenced to jail for life based solely on the word of a white person. On the other hand, the white person who made a false accusation or was accused of killing a black person usually got off with no sentence or penalty. For many people, Jim Crow laws made living life in the South even riskier. Living in fear for one's life based solely on the color of one's skin.

The stock market crashed in 1929, driving many prominent southern whites to bankruptcy and caused the inability to maintain their properties and pay their debts. This situation drove blacks who were financially dependent on their white counterparts further into financial uncertainty and decreased their ability to take care of their families. In the 1920s and 30s, a loaf of bread cost 9 cents, milk was 56 cents a gallon, eggs cost 68 cents a dozen and gasoline was 19 cents per gallon, but still making a living was difficult for black families.

Instead of being paid in cash blacks were often paid with tools, hand me down clothing or food which severely limited the type of financial resources they could accumulate. To add to the stress of the financial downturn, few blacks had cars making it necessary to walk most places. There was limited public transportation and it cost money to get to work, go shopping, and to pay bills. Just trying to survive became problematic when finances were tight.

The Roosevelt Administration created the New Deal which took place between 1933-38 to provide economic relief for unemployed/underemployed, youth and elderly. Many low-income sharecroppers and domestic workers' income were dependent on the stable income of the white plantation and business owners. After the crash of the stock market, many plantation owners lost everything and therefore were unable to maintain their primarily black workforce, which quickly became dispensable.

The New Deal provided some relief to those low-income black families who were unable to sufficiently care for their families. The New Deal also brought in the creation of entry-level jobs such as messengers, elevator, and heavy equipment operators and home delivery services. Many people, including whites, benefited from the New Deal programs. The implementation of the New Deal programs provided sharecroppers, unemployed and particularly black people the resources to leave the South and move to Northern cities. Individual jobs were available based upon skill level or the ability to learn new skills. Many people, particularly black people took advantage of the opportunity to move "Up North" to seek new opportunities.

An entire southern family would come together and choose one or two family members to venture "Up North" to find living quarters, obtain a job and save money for several months. After a time, they would send for one or two more family members who would follow the same pattern. In a few years, the entire family would be relocated to a Northern city;

cultivating a new life and fulfilling their passion and dreams.

Rev. Botts created many ministries to meet the needs of the congregation and to aid them in their personal development. He created ministries to develop children, teens, and young adults. He believed in developing positive Christian attributes, along with civic and community responsibility. He had a great love for children and was intently focused on shaping family values. He focused his ministry on teaching God's loving kindness to church members and the community. The environment was warm and welcoming, and the culture was loving and friendly. Zion quickly became the beacon of light for growth and change. Grandfather worked tirelessly to prepare his congregation to live better lives in the future.

Zion Baptist Church Leadership
1940's

Within the church structure, the elder women taught the younger women life skills such as; gardening, cooking, sewing, embroidering, crocheting, knitting, how to do hair and nails, and how to better take care of pre-school children and aging adults. The elder men taught the younger men other life skills essential to living like; hunting, fishing, car repair, and all-around handymen. They all learned and worked to become self-sufficient which many of the parishioners turned into additional sources of income (full or part-time).

Once or twice weekly, members would gather at the church and share a large meal which was prepared by the elder women. This allowed working families a couple of days per week to fellowship and work on their newly acquired craft or skill while the children received assistance with their homework and Bible study. Rev. Botts was like a father figure who molded the young women and men into mature spiritual adults who learned to work within their purpose to better the family, church, and community. Through it all, he always kept Biblical principles in front of every example he taught so everyone could recognize the power of being one with the Lord.

The friendly family-oriented environment gave Zion the reputation of being a community church. Over the years Zion provided community ministries to meet the needs of the community such as assistance with clothing, food, books, health and wellness, foreign missions and after-school programs. There were also Christian Education programs like; Sunday School, the Baptist Training Union, and numerous scholarship programs. On a daily basis, there was some form of educational development available at Zion. The Sunday School grew to over 100 children, Sunday Services attracted more than 1200 worshippers weekly, and the church was filled to capacity. Many professional people flocked to Zion bringing their expertise to the congregation. Doctors, lawyers, and business owners became a part of the fabric of the church.

Rev. and Mrs Botts Anniversary

In the book called, "<u>The History of Zion Baptist Church</u>," published in 1989 by the church's pastor and leadership, Zion was home to many distinguished musicians, choir directors, arrangers, composers, and singers. For over 30 years Mr. Willie B. Hale was the Sr. Choir Director at Zion Baptist Church. He used his musical gifts to collaborate with other local and national artists to bring performers and performances of every type of music to Minnesota and Zion Baptist Church. Included in the wide range of music offered at the church were: spirituals, hymns, gospel music, cantatas, musical plays, and Handel's Messiah. Zion was also home to quartettes, duets, men's, women's, children's choirs, as well as a young adult and gospel choirs.

When Zion was at its pinnacle, musicians local or national, made their way to come, share their gifts and talent to provide a musical experience at Zion. Notable musicians such as Dr. Reginal Buckner, Mr. Ralph Primm, Mrs. Mabel Bell, Mrs. Velma Warder, and Mrs. Barbara Green to name a few, worked along-side Mr. Hale to provide the extraordinary music experience which people still talk about today.

Many musicians came to Zion and certainly left their mark. Music was integrated into the fabric of Zion's culture and many gospel, classical, anthems and other types of music were written or arranged at Zion. The music ministry also played an important role in building Zion's reputation as being a welcoming home to many of the Twin Cities great musicians and musical performances during grandfather's tenure.

Zion Baptist Church Combined Choirs

1950s

In "<u>The History of Zion Baptist Church</u>," the leadership provides an in-depth overview of the impact that Zion Baptist Church had on the growth and development of its membership and the community during Rev. Botts reign. The book depicts the many organizational leaders, church trainers, and community outreach service providers which were available to individuals and families of the church and community. Families with children were drawn to Zion because of the multitude of activities and training that were available.

In addition, there was a strong emphasis on Christian Education training for youth and young adults. The training was geared towards the development of a firm foundation of values, beliefs, and purpose to guide them throughout their lives. There were also services where youth and young adults where prepared for the future, such as; college, jobs and life situations.

The Botts's forged strong relationships in the greater community by joining civic organizations and educational boards. They held government officials accountable for substandard housing and low wages;

supported organizations which fought against injustice through the NAACP and Urban League. They also critiqued government agencies which set policies on housing, employment, and healthcare. The Botts made sure that the black community was represented in all areas which affected their lives and welfare.

Chapter 5

SERVING GOD'S PEOPLE

There were two very different sides to my grandfather. There was the loving caring pastor who was gentle and compassionate. When I listened to him tackling problems of racial injustice in employment, housing, education or injustice in general, he became a very different person. He was intense, commanding and very determined to get his point of view across and make sure the situation was resolved, and that justice was served. He was always polite but could not be swayed and usually forced some type of agreement or concession. He was undeniably using his gifts to walk in his purpose and was not walking this journey alone. He would not give in on points which were important and could not be silenced.

He was a spirit-filled man, who knew his purpose was to break down racial barriers. These barriers prevented black people from reaching their full potential because of racial injustice and discriminatory practices. He called himself "a change agent for God," and voiced his purpose as a "leader of God's people, helping them reach higher goals."

By following the principles and practices written in the Bible he guided them to put God first, serve others second, and not be hindered by those who would try to discourage them. He used, John 10:10 *The thief cometh not, but for to steal, and to kill and to destroy I am come that they may have life, and that they might have it more abundantly,* as the biblical example. This example he taught the membership empowerment and sustainability using the rationale of not to let anyone steal you joy or dissuade you from your purpose. He always said, "human kindness will stifle ill will or poor behavior." By creating this type of environment, he developed perseverance and trust in the Lord, which fostered a healthy place for families to live, work and worship.

Under the leadership of Rev. Botts, the church membership continued to grow. He fought for black independence and black pride; always teaching others to "rely on yourself God has already given you everything you need; you will want to listen, then follow the directions which will be provided to you." "By following these steps, you will always be ready to put your resources to work." As a sought- after preacher, speaker, and leader, Rev. Botts mobilized crowds of people and taught them to hold public officials accountable and assume accountability for those who are unable to speak for themselves.

The parishioners all learned to work together, support each other and the church. They worked and worshipped together as one large community. Many families, with more than two generations of family members in Minnesota, came from Missouri and were from the same area where my grandfather grew up. They had many celebrations commemorating their move from Missouri to Minnesota.

They rejoiced in the growth and wellbeing of their families and the opportunities to have positions which keep them moving forward. A wonderful example of black family migration tells the story of Albert Allen's family, the first of five generations who moved "Up North" for a better future. The genealogy was documented in 2014 to a DVD and is titled "The

<u>family of Albert Allen</u>," which is currently housed at the Minnesota Historical Society.

Rev. Botts led the church and its congregation of parishioners through many difficult times. He led them through racial injustice and poor economic times of the 1930s. Racial injustice still existed in the '40s, when World War II broke out. Many of the community's young black men signed up to go to war, and racial injustice and prejudice were prevalent there also. While many of the same conditions still existed in the '50s, he kept parishioners motivated to work and resolve their own problems and not look to others for solutions. Historically, Zion Baptist Church was the largest church in the black community when grandfather was the pastor.

He and other community leaders, who were a part of his inner circle, worked with the local community leaders; such as former Directors, W. Gertrude Brown and Henry Thomas of Phyliss Wheatley Settlement House. The role of the organization was to provide temporary housing and safe recreation for children and adults. Grandfather and other community leaders worked diligently with the NAACP and the Urban League on issues of equal justice in education and housing. He worked with Anthony Cassius and Nellie Stone Johnson on disputes with local labor unions concerning equality in pay and benefits.

He was often called upon to work with city mayors and state governors to work through situations of inequity and injustice. As the pastor and spokesperson of the largest black church in the community, his fight against discrimination thrust him into the forefront of the racial and ethnic divide. It was in those situations that he earned the reputation for being a change agent because his ability to bring compromise to difficult situations meant that both sides became winners.

Grandfather was the State Moderator of the National Baptist Convention for many years. His responsibilities were to organize a systematic approach to pray, plan and enhance the unity of the people; facing issues at the local, district, state and national levels. He was often called upon by pastors and officials in other states to help relieve racial tension because his negotiation skills were also recognized and celebrated within the convention.

The church grew rapidly during the 40s and 50s and the growth was effectively managed. It was important to establish several new committees to accommodate the growth and keep everyone involved in ministry work. The Rooms Committee was one of the new committees which was established so each member of the committee would be responsible for the upkeep of the church.

The committee's roles were to clean the room and ensure that relevant materials were available in the room. In addition, the appropriate number of volunteers were to be assigned to the rooms when in use. This process provided members the opportunity to feel like they were contributing to the success of the church. The Official Board was expanded to be responsible for business planning in addition to being responsible for the oversight of church operations and committee activities. Many individuals and families greatly contributed their time, gifts and talents to the success of Zion Baptist Church.

Early parishioners contributed much to the life of the church. Lucille Levels was the Church Clerk at Zion for several years dating back to 1929. She was responsible for recording the church's ministry activities, financial reports, and action items that were presented at the church business meetings. She tracked and reported most of the official business of the church including the number of members and the status of their membership.

Approximately 2 years ago a friend that I had not seen in 25 years called me to say she found something that would be very dear to me. When she arrived, she handed me one of my grandfather's Bibles with his signature and date clearly visible on the front page. In addition, there was a church ledger written and dated 1929 by Ms. Levels. She was very dedicated to them and worked tirelessly to serve them as their assistant both at home and at the church. She had no other family and so they became her family. She was a kind and caring woman who always bought me the prettiest dresses when I was a small child and would always bring me treats. She lived with Aunt Ella (grandfather's youngest daughter) Uncle Bob and Sylvester (Ella's husband and son) until her passing in 1949.

Bertha Smith was a pillar at Zion Baptist Church. She came to Zion after graduating from high school. She worked in virtually every ministry in the church. She was a special needs teacher and worked tirelessly to support the health and wellbeing of the church. She was instrumental in bringing many people into the church to become members.

She had many great stories about grandfather and grandmother because she did not drive and often rode with them. One of her favorite stories about grandfather was, one day they were going downtown to the bank with her in the backseat of the car and grandfather was driving erratically, as usual, all over the road.

A police officer pulled him over and stopped him in the middle of downtown Minneapolis at 7th and Nicollet. The officer told him that he was driving across the center line and if he did not stop, he was going to take his license away from him. Grandfather smiled and replied, "Sir, it is rude for me to talk to Ms. Smith with my back turned to her." The officer pleaded, "Rev. Botts please stay off my street or I will have to take your driver's license away from you." Grandfather never stopped driving down 7th Street to the bank and the police never bothered him again. Aunt Bertha believed the police officer requested a transfer from that location so he would not have to encounter Rev. Botts. After she'd tell the story, she would laugh and laugh about that incident.

Bertha was a loving person and did much good for many people including my grandfather and grandmother. She was loved and respected by everyone at Zion. As the oldest of her God daughters, I was given the privilege of singing one of her favorite songs, "The Greatest of These is Love," at her homegoing service in 2014.

Grandfather and grandmother always had various members from church taking extra good care of them. One such person was Raymond Cooper who was an accountant and held several positions in the church before becoming the Chair of the Trustees Board where he served for several years. He was a kind, quiet man with a big smile and laughing eyes. Once he retired, he became their personal driver. He'd drive them to the National Baptist Conventions around the country. Planning to travel was a lot of work because black folks could not eat at restaurants, stay in hotels or use public facilities for water or bathroom breaks. Also, there were cities or parts of cities where blacks could not be seen after dark without severe consequences. Grandmother would start planning months before the scheduled trip to make sure they would be safe, and someone would be expecting them at each juncture of the trip.

She would use a map to chart out the roads they would take from one city to the next. She plotted out everything, bathroom breaks, lunch, dinner stops and where they would sleep for the night. Grandmother was amazing, she had phone numbers and addresses of people from across the country. When she called, they all seemed to know her and would set up whatever she asked. She made sure each trip was safe and there where people looking out for them. They always stayed with families, never in hotels and rarely ate in restaurants. The country was still very segregated, and she took a lot of care to ensure their trips would be safe and they could come and go as necessary to perform their duties.

Front Row: Rev. Botts, John Blackman, and Mrs. Botts,
Second Row: Willie B. Hale, Carrie Hale, Bertha Smith, and
Raymond Cooper
National Baptist Convention in St. Louis MO 1948

Mr. Cooper got so much joy out of being with my grandparents. Many of the old southern sayings and the tag team banter they used with each other kept him in constant stitches. When he was tickled, everyone around him was tickled. He'd begin to laugh silently and put his hands over his mouth and before he knew it tears were running down his face because he was trying to control himself and hold back the laughter. When the tears came, and he was still laughing silently, he looked so funny he made everyone else laugh. As everyone else began to laugh he'd erupt into loud laughter which would have people laughing nonstop for several minutes.

These stories portray the warm loving environment and culture which was created by the leaders of Zion Baptist Church. There was a culture of service and caring for one another that created a bond between the people which grew into long-lasting relationships. Everyone truly loved and cared for each other. Zion was like a family even when there were disagreements, they learned from Rev. Botts to resolve the issue in love and not allow any disagreements to break that bond.

My maternal grandmother, Juanita London was another one of the early migrants to come to Minnesota. She and her two young daughters, Juanda the oldest also my mother, and Louise migrated from Satin, Texas to rural Minnesota for a few years before settling in North Minneapolis and joining Zion Baptist Church in approximately 1928. After their arrival, Juanita met and married Dayton Cuff and they had three daughters, Jacqueline, Donna, and Dora. The five girls grew up in North Minneapolis, attended Zion Baptist Church and graduated from North High School in the 1940s' and '50s. They were actively involved in sports at school and at Sumner Field along with continuous engagements at Phyllis Wheatley Settlement House.

Grandmother was one of the true examples of Rev. Botts teachings. She loved everyone and lived a life of service until the day she died. Grandmother Juanita cooked for some of the richest families and festivals in Texas before moving to Minnesota. Wherever she lived she was always put in charge of running the kitchen and directing the kitchen staff. It was no wonder when she arrived in Minneapolis and attended Zion, one of the first things they found out about her was her ability and passion for cooking. During her lifetime she cooked continuously for the church, many social events and family get-togethers.

Seven days a week, no matter the time of day, whenever you arrived at Grandmother Juanita's house, the aroma of turkey and dressing, beef roast, freshly baked yeast rolls, apple pie, cherry pie, greens, sweet potatoes, macaroni and cheese, okra and anything you could possibly want to eat filled the air and would meet you at the door. Everyone loved Sunday dinners at Grandmother Juanita's house. The house was always packed every Sunday after church. The guests would come to enjoy the fabulous food and personalized service. Her most frequent guests were Rev. and Mrs. Botts. She loved to attend to them, and they loved being invited to take part in the fellowship.

The protocol of those times dictated that the children ate last. My mother used to tell me that she, her sisters and cousins were never worried about "Mama" as they called her, running out of food; there was always enough of everything to eat when it was their turn to sit down at the table. The one thing the younger family members did not like was being the "cleanup crew." After they finished with their meals, they were to clear the table, wash and dry the dishes, clean the stove, sweep, mop the floor and take out the trash. Every day, the house was always returned to its original clean condition in order to be ready for the next day of cooking.

If you arrived at Grandmother Juanita's house during the week there was always plenty of food on the stove. Whether you were hungry or not, you'd want to eat because you could smell the wonderful food. Your taste buds would demand a sample of something, even if it was only a slice of pie because food was always offered to you. No one could drop by Grandmother Juanita's house without having a bite to eat. Preparing and serving food and people was her ministry, passion and she lovingly fulfilled her role throughout her life.

A generation later, one of my fondest memories of being at grandmother's house was the quarterly mother/daughter brunch. Grandmother would cook something that was special to each of her grandchildren and have the biggest spread imaginable and it was ready when we walked through the door. It was like Sunday dinner but better because she did all that work for us. We could eat, laugh and play until she prepared the luncheon/dinner food for guests who frequently dropped by. Once the food was prepared and safely stored away from the kitchen, she would call her five older granddaughters to the kitchen to "DO" our hair.

The ritual was our mothers would wash our hair at home then bring us to grandmothers for the food festivities, followed by grandmother "DOING" our hair. She straightened our hair with a hot straightening comb as she had done for her daughters when they were our age. The only difference was that grandmother was older now and she would begin to tire after the second or third child.

Being the oldest granddaughter, I learned very quickly to be the first one in the chair when grandmother called us to the kitchen so not to be the one in the chair when she began to tire or needed to answer the phone. When that happened there was a potential for you to get burned with that hot comb. Once that happened you would remember and not want it to happen again. I became smart very quick.

I also remember the times when my mother and her sisters would take us kids to the movies followed by dinner at either the Nankin Chinese Restaurant or The Forum; an "all you could eat" restaurant which were their favorites in downtown Minneapolis. As children, this was a big deal for us because we could wear our church dresses for these rare outings to go downtown and spend the day with our mothers.

Inadvertently, we would run into other church families who were having the same experience as we were, and they seemed very happy. I remember feeling so grown-up and proud to be able to enjoy that type of recreation. Somehow, I knew that many blacks, even a few black families from Zion Church, where not in a position to take their children on outings like this one.

Chapter 6

STRENGTHENING COMMUNITIES

My father, Reverend Henry W. Botts, Jr., was the son of Rev. Botts, Sr. He met my mother Juanda Cuff when he moved to Minneapolis from Chicago in 1943. They began to date after she completed high school and fell in love. They were married in 1945 having a small wedding ceremony at Zion Baptist Church. Two months after I was born in 1946, my father was called to pastor St. John's Baptist Church in Sioux Falls, South Dakota. I am the third generation to be born after slavery; the first generation to be born "Up North" and the last person to carry the surname Botts in Minnesota.

St. John's Baptist Church was a small black church located a few blocks from downtown Sioux Falls with an adjoining two-bedroom parsonage. There were about 40 families that belonged to the church and we all become very close. Sioux Falls had a small black population and several of the families were headed by retired military men who served at the Air Force Base and remained in the city following their tour of duty.

There were a lot of social gatherings like picnics and dinners among the church members because Sioux Falls was a small rural town and did not have many family activities. I remember that most of the family outings consisted of going to the water-fall, "Bells", the ice cream shop, the movie theater or drive-in. Being an only child, I loved the larger gatherings with other children.

My father was very busy developing and growing the church. He and the church leaders worked constantly to restore the church which had fallen into disrepair. He was active in the community and worked with city leaders to find ways to put Sioux Falls on the map as a countryside vacation spot. People from communities near and far could visit and explore the city, parks, and countryside. There were a lot of firsts for blacks in the Sioux Falls Community during our stay; some were able to work at the post office and others worked on railroad jobs.

Several nationally renowned black musicians and civic leaders came to Sioux Falls to perform and hold rallies. They stayed at our house and houses of our parishioners because they were not allowed to stay in hotels. Many of those events, along with reoccurring church events, were covered in the Minneapolis Spokesman-Recorder because there was no black newspaper in Sioux Falls.

My father and the church leaders canvased the community to determine the needs and to ensure that the church was meeting those needs. They identified several needs where the church provided new programs. By introducing a day time bible study and small lunch they were able to reach the senior community who lacked the stamina to fix two meals every day and preferred not to attend evening gatherings. There was a need for an after-school program to accommodate the children of working parents. My mother worked very hard on this program each evening. She would make the sandwiches, mix up Kool-Aid, get chips and bake cakes for dessert. This was a joy for me because I'd have several hours per week to interact with other children and make friends.

In the fall, the church held a bowling tournament and the entire church would show up to cheer for their favorite team. With the continuing summer picnics and the men going hunting every fall, the church became a real community where we all worked and worshiped. I could not imagine a better place to grow up. Children were free to go to each other houses, play on the school playground or visit the neighboring farmer's cows and horses.

In 1947 my father enrolled in Sioux Falls College; a Christian college where he completed his Bachelor of Science Degree in Sociology with a minor in German. My mother was the church musician who played the piano and directed both the children and adult choirs. Mother also studied at Sioux Falls College to become a classical musician. She became quite accomplished and gave several concerts which raised money for Saint John's Church. She also loved to return to Minneapolis and participate as one of the musical accompanists for the large annual concert which was held at Zion Baptist Church to support chosen charities.

She had a love for fine clothes and was 5'9", with a small frame and she looked like a movie star with her long slender body and long flowing hair. I loved to watch my mother dress as she prepared to leave the house because she never left one detail of perfection undone. She was beautiful from head to toe, but she never seemed to notice.

The way she prepared herself to leave the house was ingrained in her from her childhood; to always look your best because you never knew who's watching. Whether that is true, I don't know, but I do know she took great care to look her best. Then she would go to visit the sick and get down on her hands and knees and scrub their floors, wash their clothes or bathe them. It did not matter how much time she had spent making sure she looked impeccable. She was humble, giving and loving. She was a servant who lived to love and serve others.

One day she decided to apply to work at an upscale dress shop in downtown Sioux Falls. The manager was shocked to have a black woman applying for a job at a downtown store. After they talked, she decided to offer mother a part-time position ironing the clothes and dressing the manikins. Mother always laughed and said, "I'm sure she thought no one would see me because I'd be out of the customer's sight. I was hired to work afternoons and evenings after the store closed." Then dad would laugh and say, "honey they can't miss you, look at you!"

Her ability to coordinate fashion and fabrics far surpassed the other sales-women which caused the customers to begin to ask for the lady who dressed the manikins. The customers did not hesitate to ask her to coordinate their outfits once they placed their eyes on her. Because of her beauty, grace, and sense of fashion, she had quite a following and attracted many fashion-conscious women to the store.

Mrs. Juanda Botts

Mother was still studying to become a classical musician and working at the dress shop when she became ill and was diagnosed with Lupus. She was one of the earliest Lupus diagnoses. There were no approved medications or treatments for her at that time. She struggled desperately to maintain her composure and continue playing music and displaying fashions which gave her so much joy. Eventually, my father made the decision to move the family back to Minneapolis where she could get the best medical treatment and be close to family and friends who could help him take care of her.

I was sad to learn that we needed to leave the beautiful wide-open panoramic scene of Sioux Falls with the beautiful parks, lakes and a waterfall you could stare at for hours. As a child in Sioux Falls, my life was free, safe and uncomplicated. As children, we could leave home in the morning and romp through the parks, fields or farms all day with no restrictions. I knew all that would change when we moved back to the hustle and bustle of Minneapolis, which to me was a very big city.

Being in Sioux Falls for eight years, my father and mother had made many friends and acquaintances all of who attended the farewell ceremony held at the church. Government and civic leaders read proclamations noting his great work and spoke about the energy and enthusiasm Rev. Botts Jr. had brought to make the community a better place for all to live. Choirs from the Twin Cities and Sioux Falls College came to sing jubilant songs of praises to God for the abundant blessings the community had received. It was a day of great sharing and celebration and a memorable day!

Chapter 7

CHANGING LIVES

When we returned to Minneapolis, Zion Baptist Church was still the leading black church in Minneapolis. By today's standards Zion could have been considered a megachurch with more than 1200 members and many large families representing two or three generations living in Minnesota. Even today when people find out that I'm a Botts, they let me know that Rev. Botts baptized or christened them, married their parents or buried their grandparents. They always recall the year and make a point of letting me know how special that event was in their lives. That was the impact my grandfather had on people no matter their station in life. He was a loving, warm and captivating man who always left a lasting impression.

The Northside of Minneapolis was a very diverse community. All the children attended the same schools regardless of their ethnicity. The rich and poor lived harmoniously in the same community. Many of the black families and low-income white families lived in the projects or other substandard housing units. They looked out for one another, even correcting each other's children when they were misbehaving. Many of the church members lived in the neighborhood which surrounded the church.

During that same period of time, America joined World War II, it was the early '40s, and many of the young community men went to war. Some of those men came from black families and churches in the Twin Cities. During this time the black people who were not active in the war were able to get good paying jobs at the Twin Cities Army Ammunitions Plant. With so many of the men gone off to war women were eventually able to get jobs outside of the home and work at the ammunition plant. This was the first time many black women received a consistent full-time paycheck which enabled them to care for their families while their husbands were away.

Black folks made more money during this time because every able-bodied person was asked to work to support the war. When the war ended in 1945 the situation changed. The ammunition plant was slated to close and many workers were laid off. A lot of the women were asked to give up their employment and go back to the home so the men returning from war could have jobs.

Again, the church became a haven, the place for the displaced, a place where all were welcome. The church was the place to come to have your needs met. Families felt welcome and were a part of something greater than themselves. They could see hope and trust through others who were there to help them. Most importantly they were always treated with dignity and respect. That was the type of community that Rev. and Mrs. Botts created at Zion Baptist Church.

My grandparents lived in the church parsonage at 19th and Lyndale. In the quiet of the afternoon when grandmother was busy with her responsibilities at the church, grandfather would tell me the stories of his early years. Somehow at a young age, I felt privileged to spend time listening to my grandfather's stories. I never heard him tell these stories to anyone else, not even his son, my father.

After all the years my Grandfather had been away from Meadville and his upbringing, he never forgot the feeling of not having new clothes and being ashamed of the condition of the clothes he had to wear. In our conversations, he'd still mention the feeling of dirt and grit on his skin and how he'd brush and brush his clothes trying to remove the residue of memories when he was young.

Many times, I could feel his vulnerability as he talked about being hungry or sent into the fields to hunt rabbits and squirrels for dinner and finding a freshly hung body of a black man or boy hanging from a tree. He'd talk about how he would hide for long periods of time to ensure that no one returned and see him knowing he could have been next.

Sometimes his voice would crack when he'd recall the number of families who lost their land and their livelihood because of the loss of a family member. It was painful for him to recall the lack of compassion shown by the landowners and bankers who were responsible for the debt collection. He would share how they would show up at the family's door with a letter evicting them immediately. Many of his dreams to become a minister of the gospel and serving people in need started then.

His early life experiences fully prepared him for life's journey and the purpose he was to fulfill. He experienced firsthand the lasting effects of racial injustice, intolerance and white supremacy. He experienced the anger, fear, and degradation towards black people. He also knew the God he served would make a way for the people who were followers and believed in the written word. That's how he began shaping his own purpose and goals to become a man of God, a change agent, a messenger and a leader for the Lord.

I remember asking him how he was able to determine his life's goal at such an early age. He responded, "in the community where I lived ministers were the only black men who wore suits every day and were respected by everyone. They weren't persecuted but were treated with dignity." He said he wanted to be a well-regarded minister making his father proud of him. He knew all the agony, hurt and pain his father had gone through having lived most of his life in the strongholds of slavery.

As he studied the men, he found them to be more than preachers and teachers of the gospel. They were activists fighting on the front lines of the aftermath of slavery and persecution. The black churches because of their sovereign status were exempt from the white protestant rule and became independent organizations. By creating their own structures and rules it allowed them to become autonomous houses of worship. The churches afforded their membership the freedom to worship in their own way but also became havens and safe houses for underground railroad travelers.

He learned that the ministers were comforters who held the hands of widows and children whose husbands and fathers had gone into town for supplies and were killed for some unknown reason. He saw those men as the protectors of the black community and the black church. He could see that they were God-centered, fearless men, who answered the call to guide, direct and protect the people of God through very turbulent times; and that became his goal.

That discovery set him on a path of determination and preparation where he could see himself as a future minister caring for people and fighting against racism and injustices in the black community. He accepted the role of being a servant of God and a shepherd for the people. He spent his entire life perfecting his skills in four areas; his character, purpose, relationship with God, and becoming an outstanding carrier of the Gospel of Jesus Christ. He also said he wanted to be an example for youth in the community. Grandfather and his siblings learned to be strong Christian men and women, to respect others, and expect respect in return. They were also taught to seek freedom in the world and not be held back by condemnation and discrimination.

When I was growing up grandfather still shined his shoes every night, wore a 3-piece suit, collared shirt, tie or bow tie every day. During the winter he'd always wear a top coat and dress hat, and I never saw him wear any type of casual clothing. When we would dress to go out of the house, he was always looked impeccable from his shoes and ties to his horn-rimmed glasses and hat. From the time I was born until I grew out of children's shoes, he always bought my Christmas and Easter Shoes from the Buster Brown Shoe Store in downtown Minneapolis. Every season when we walked in the door he'd say, "nothing but the best for my girl, nothing but the best."

Grandfather had so many old country expressions that used to make me laugh, and this one really cracked me up. Once dressed, he'd look in the mirror and say, "I'm cleaner than the board of health," then smile at himself and give me that funny little wink. When I was a little girl, he was still getting up at 4:00 a.m. to study for two hours before he started his daily routine. You could say he had limited formal schooling, but he was one of the most brilliant and eloquent men I've ever known. I felt grandfather and I could talk about anything based on all the information he shared with me over the years.

He shared his innermost thoughts and memories with me when I was between the ages of 9 and 15. I felt like I was his secret confidant. He would share the things that might make him seem weak or vulnerable to other people because he knew I loved him and just wanted to be with him. I had no thought or opinion about what he said; it was just a privilege to spend quality time in his presence. Maybe it was his way of taking my mind off my mother's serious illness and her ongoing doctor's appointments and hospital stays. These talks continued almost a year past my mother's untimely death at the age of 36 when she succumbed to Lupus.

After my mother passed neither dad or I seemed to have any passion or purpose. He worked for the Curtis Hotel and the Minneapolis Club as a waiter and I continued with school. The only thing that kept him going was labor disputes over wages and benefits and the ongoing union protests that grandfather organized through the churches. For a few months' life was just a blur, days came and went, nothing seemed important until my dad was notified by the church that they were planning a big community celebration to commemorate grandfather's retirement.

Suddenly we had a lot of work to accomplish. We needed to identify the people and organizations that he had worked with locally and nationally in order to enact the story of his life. We were asked to identify his favorite song, bible verses, and favorite foods. Basically, they wanted to know everything we could remember about him as a man, a family man and the pastor of Zion Baptist Church so they could fully depict the story of his life.

I knew the name of grandfather's favorite song, it was "Blessed Assurance." That hymn is still sung around the world today and one of the places where it can be found is in the New National Baptist Hymnal printed June 1982, pg. 27, by Fanny J. Crosby and Phoebe P. Knapp. The song lyrics are: *"Blessed Assurance, Jesus is mine! O what a foretaste of glory divine! Heir of salvation, purchased of God, Born of His Spirit, and I'm washed in blood. Oh, this is my story, this is my song, praising my Savior all the day long. Oh, oh, oh, This is my story, this is my song, and I'm praising my Savior all the day long.*" He would sing it all the time. The song which soothed his soul or lifted his spirits was penned two years before his birth in 1873. Whether he was happy, sad, up, or down, and needed that internal connection (a heart-to-heart talk with God), he would sing, hum, or moan that song from morning 'til night.

Chapter 8

FULFILLING LIFE'S PURPOSE

Grandfather, now in his 90s, had surpassed the appointed time of retirement because of his exuberance for the church and the life of its people. But now the time had come for him to retire and the church was planning a celebration of his life which was to take place in June 1959. In the weeks leading up to his retirement, there were special luncheons given by Phyliss Wheatley House and the Urban League commemorating his years of dedicated service.

He was hailed as one of the Twin Cities greatest leaders who stood for justice and equality for all and who fought against discrimination, unfair labor practices and substandard housing in the black community. He was interviewed on the local radio and television stations who announced his retirement. They covered many of the contributions he had made to the Twin Cities community, particularly North Minneapolis during the 30-years he spent at Zion Baptist Church. He was recognized as being a scholarly gentleman who successfully led the church and community through years of turmoil, change, and growth.

On the day of the celebration, there was so much excitement in the air. As people poured into the church you could see and feel the love and respect the community had for my grandfather. It was the most outstanding send-off celebration commemorating his years of service that I had ever seen. In attendance were churches, pastors, and choirs both local and national. There were so much singing and so many commemorative speeches that the event went on for hours, but nobody seemed to notice. It was a very joyous occasion and the entire twin cities community took part in the event.

The mayor and governor's offices were represented. There were representatives of every major organization in the Twin Cities including every organizational board on which he had served. To name a few there was the Ministerial Alliance, Minneapolis Council of Churches, National Baptist Convention, Minneapolis State Baptist Convention, Phyliss Wheatley, the Urban League, NAACP, and the press.

The paragraph that touched me so deeply in the Retirement Testimonial Program

Booklet read:

The love of this shepherd for his people has held the church together and built a firm foundation of spiritual depth. Surely, Rev. Botts has shown us the Father. It has been the guiding principles of his ministry, to preach the Word of God, in and out of season. Our hearts are touched by his departure, but our lives have been enriched by his presence. I will never forget the love and outpouring of gratitude shown to my grandparents throughout the years of their tenure and especially during the celebratory tribute.

Testimonial Program
of
REVEREND HENRY WILSON BOTTS, SR.

1929   1959

REV. H. W. BOTTS SR.

"I have preached righteousness in the great congregation"
"Lo, I have not refrained my lips. O Lord, thou knowest"

ZION BAPTIST CHURCH

1023 N. LYNDALE AVE., MINNEAPOLIS, MINN.

Sunday, June 21, 1959

Morning Service 11:00   Afternoon 4:00

Rev. Henry W. Botts Sr.
Retirement Celebration

As fate would have it, later in the year, Zion Baptist Church was slated for demolition by the City of Minneapolis. An Urban Renewal project to bring highway 94 through the north side of Minneapolis had been approved. This meant Zion would need to relocate and build a new church. Several years before his retirement Rev. Botts had started a building fund to either fix or replace the current structure.

Zion was a very large old building that needed an extensive overhaul, or it would have to be replaced if it were to meet the new city codes and serve as a public place of worship. After a full assessment, it was determined, based upon the cost of renovation that the demolition should proceed. Zion Church would build a new structure. The earth-shattering news was bittersweet for many people who had shared a lifetime of joy and sorrow with each other while growing up and learning to live, love and care for each other as taught by Rev. Botts. It was very hard for the community to accept the fact that Zion Baptist Church, a beacon of life, hope and strength in the community, would be torn down and replaced by a freeway. The very nature of the freeway was to quickly move people from downtown to the suburbs by going around North Minneapolis and not drive through the area and enjoy its history, diversity, and contributions to the City of Minneapolis.

The unfortunate circumstances of needing to demolish the old Zion led to an opportunity to build a new Zion Baptist Church to carry on the history and legacy of all who had come before. In honoring the past, grandfather was asked to break the ground and throw the first shovel of dirt at the new location. He is pictured in <u>The History of Zion Baptist Church Booklet</u> at the ground-breaking ceremony. The new structure would be located at 621 Elwood Avenue North, Minneapolis MN.

After the years of dedicated service to Zion Baptist Church retirement did not suit grandfather well and his health began to fail. He was in his 90s and had a hard time adjusting to the change of no longer overseeing the church and its parishioners. Grandmother was his caretaker, but she was close to 90 herself and not in the best of health either. He could not find enough things of interest to fill his days and it seemed as if he was lost. For the first time in his life, he had no purpose to drive him.

**Rev. Henry Botts and Sis. Hester Sudduth
Ground-Breaking Ceremony for the New Zion Baptist Church**

He started having health issues; first high blood pressure then two mild heart attacks back to back. The heart attacks took a lot out of him and left him feeling very weak. He started to withdraw and often stayed to himself and didn't engage with others.

By this time, I was in high school and just old enough to drive. I lived with my Aunt Ella and Uncle Bob and was given the privilege of taking my grandparents wherever they needed to go. Of course, I was very thrilled to have the opportunity to drive the car so frequently. I would take them to the doctor, the store or church several times per week. Grandfather would always perk up when I came around. He loved to tell me stories about how things were when he grew up and I loved to hear the stories because I was his greatest fan. But after chauffeuring them around for a couple of months the calls came less and less.

On a bright October day, I received a call from my Aunt Ella urging me to come to the hospital because my grandfather had just had another heart attack and all the family was all on their way to learn about his condition. In the short time it took me to reach the hospital he had already gone home to glory. He had received his final call from destiny and with this last heart attack, his life was over. But what I saw when I looked at him was a slight smile which let me know that he was at peace and everything was alright. He had fought the good fight and was now ready to be with the Lord because it was time for him to rest and enjoy the rewards of his labor.

The news of his death signaled the end of an era and the end of the life of one of the north side's most beloved public figures. He was revered and loved because of the way he lived his life and shared the love of God. Rev. Henry W. Botts Sr., passed away in October 1967. His service was the first homegoing service to be held at the new Zion Baptist Church, and what a celebration of life they had for him.

My grandfather had fulfilled the purpose that was given him by God in his youth, with his ministerial work was now complete. His life and ministry brought love, peace, comfort, growth, and stability to Zion Baptist

Church and the North Minneapolis community for 30 years. As a Christian believer, I know that his life did not end here because he used his time on earth to set up a legacy of teaching others how to live life victoriously through Jesus Christ. The legacy that he lived and taught others to duplicate followed the same examples that Christ taught in the Bible.

From an early age, grandfather studied the Bible in earnest. His focus was not about how he could become famous or earn a lot of money, but his intent on being one with God, the Creator of the Heavens and the Earth, was paramount. There was something within that made him know he was connected to the Heavenly Father and God would care for him all of his days. He studied, prayed and meditated until he cultivated having the faith of a mustard seed. Through the ongoing relationship with God, he could set aside his cares, worry's and fears because he knew God was with him always. The belief in God and the faith to walk independently set him apart from his peers and made him a true follower and a person that other people wanted to imitate.

As he continued to grow in reverence and worship with God, he started to seek his purpose. As he looked around his community for signs of who he was to become he saw black men like him, who wore suits, were treated fairly by all races and they were ministers.

Through his studies and meditation, he learned very quickly the necessity of being a person of good character and being a person above reproach. He learned that character is known as the combined total of a person's inner thoughts, beliefs, values, and attitudes. Character is the total essence of a person. In order to be an authentic leader of Gods people, grandfather saw the need to focus on making sure his character was parallel to his purpose.

Grandfather's purpose was to be a vessel where God could work through him to provide strength and guidance to the people and have a positive impact on how blacks were looked upon. For the betterment of Gods people, he was guided to confront racism, discriminatory treatment and injustice. Grandfather and many others of his time became the voice of the people. They brought the injustices and inequities to light and held those who were accountable for their beliefs and actions.

He and the ministers before him were the front-runners of the work of Dr. Martin Luther King who was eventually able to bring national/international attention to the plight of the disenfranchised. That action, fueling the passing of the Civil Rights Act of 1964, ended segregation in public places and banned employment discrimination. It is considered one of the greatest legislative achievements of the civil rights movement.

When I think about the circle of life, which the Collins Dictionary describes as; "nature's way of taking and giving back life to earth. It symbolizes the universe being sacred and divine and represents the infinite nature of energy; meaning if something dies it gives new life to another." I can see that the universe is connected from the beginning of time and as human beings we are part of that cycle and connected to one another. This connectivity imposes a level of responsibility and accountability to create positive outcomes to situations and actions which affected the universe.

This train of thought leads me to believe that human beings are to be accountable for one another just as animals, birds, trees, flowers, etc. are responsible for their species. Shouldn't one of the human beings' primary responsibilities be to learn and understand their purpose; why they exist in the world and what they are to achieve during their time on earth? It seems that fewer and fewer people realize they are in the world to accomplish a goal and understand there is a purpose for their life.

God showed me how the writing of this book would lead me to my next purpose which now has become crystal clear. My husband, Gerald, is a Minister. We created and dedicated a teaching ministry in the '90s as a part of our wedding vows. Gerald and I have been praying for a way to bring grandfather's legacy to life and share with others the methods he used to build success. We have raised our children, retired from corporate work and traveled the world teaching others the love of Jesus Christ and the transforming powers of his ministry.

We now have the vision for phase two of our ministry which is to prepare people to serve others by providing solutions. As we begin our new journey, we are proud to be able to focus our attention on creating new methods to help people thrive by following Gods word.

My grandfather's legacy reaches far beyond his life and teaching. It is embedded in me and others of my generation and now I have the opportunity to share his legacy through the stories of his life. The writing of this book is having a profound impact on my life. I'm gaining new insights and wisdom every day. Now I am anxious to pass the teaching of grandfather's life on to others.

The examples of putting others first, making sure their needs are met, exuding love and expecting love in return demonstrates how my grandfather used his faith and belief in God to touch and change people's lives everywhere he went. His life is a true testimony of how an ordinary man can do extraordinary work by trusting and believing in God. My prayer is that by telling his story we will ignite a flame in the hearts of young men and women to seek their purpose and live life victoriously by living under the Will of the Father.

"When Destiny Calls" will you be ready? Will You Live your Life with Purpose?

Matthew 5:16 Let your light so shine before men, that they may see your good works, and glorify your Father which is in heaven.

ZION BAPTIST CHURCH
621 Elwood Avenue, North
Completed and dedicated in September 1967

Epilogue

My Grandfather, Rev. Henry Botts Sr's., story is a clear demonstration of one humble man's accomplishments because he dared to believe in the Almighty God. He believed continuous study and preparation would guide him and his family to great success as shown in the Bible. The positive impact of his service to the church and communities was felt by everyone he touched from Missouri to Minnesota. He was a timeless man; who could relate to humanity and the focus on helping others shaped his entire life and legacy.

In 1996, my husband Rev. Gerald Garth and I founded Dove Ministries a faith-based organization. We were inspired by grandfathers example of helping others and we focused our mission on strengthening the family unit.

This is critical teaching for the faith-based community which seeks to reclaim misplaced individuals and families. The teaching will provide the alignment between current and future generations strengthening the unity and faith walk in our community.

COMMUNITY REFLECTIONS

Pastor Botts brought stability and sound teaching to Zion Baptist church during his ministry. He was a gentleman who everyone loved. As an elder in the church when my family arrived, Rev Botts was an encourager to my father, Pastor Emeritus Curtis Herron who was called as the second pastor after his retirement. Zion Baptist Church is pleased to host the community book launch celebration of "When Destiny Calls" the biography of Rev. Henry Botts Sr., tenure following the great depression of 1929.

Pastor Brian Herron Sr.

HISTORIC RELATIONSHIP BETWEEN PILGRIM BAPTIST CHURCH ZION BAPTIST CHURCH & THE REVEREND HENRY BOTTS, SR.

The core of Minnesota's African-American history and culture can be found on both sides of the Mississippi River dating as far back as the 1800s with the St. Anthony community in Minneapolis and St. Paul in the state's capital city. It is within this historical/ geographical context that we find, in approximately 1878, one of the first actions the Rev. Robert Hickman took once becoming Pilgrim Baptist Church's official pastor, that being to establish Zion Mission (later to become Zion Baptist Church) in Minneapolis. This is the legacy of the Rev. Henry Botts, Sr. who served 30 years (1929-1959) as Zion's 8th Senior Pastor. Though the Rev. Henry Botts, Sr. was before my arrival to the

Twin Cities, I did have the pleasure of being introduced to him by proxy through many conversations with his namesake, the Rev. Henry Botts, Jr., who served as my retired associate at Pilgrim Baptist Church. Through his poetic genius and gift for storytelling like that of a griot, I learned much of the African-American history of the Twin Cities. Though separated by the twists and turns of the mighty Mississippi the history of Zion and Pilgrim Baptist are eternally woven together.

Rev. Charles L. Gill, D. Min., Senior Pastor

Pilgrim Baptist Church

St. Paul, MN

I remember "Old Zion," on Lyndale Avenue North. There was a child-friendly Sunday School where we all learned and grew together. My teacher was Mrs. Clara Pettiford. I lived around the corner on Aldrich Avenue. I remember a huge hump at the back of the church where we as kids loved to play. One Sunday in October of 1957 following his sermon, Rev Henry Botts Sr., asked if there was anyone who wanted to ask

Jesus to come into their heart so they could be saved. All of us young folks sat in the back of the church, and I remember nudging my friend and saying, "I want to go up there. Come on and go with me." I went forward and later was baptized. My Sunday School teacher was very happy for me. Those were the days!"

Rev., Dr. Harvey D. Witherspoon Jr.

Mrs. Hester Sudduth served with Rev. Botts Sr. for many years as Chair of the Trustee Board. She was very active in the church's affairs. She had deep regard for Rev. Botts and most of her children and grandchildren attended Zion. The Suddath's and the Wilson's were relatives and could fill a half section of the church for Sunday service. The church was a child-friendly environment where we were nurtured and taught the word of God. We also spent much time together as families going to parks, other churches, and family dinners. Rev. Botts was like a grandfather to us. He was loving and kind and participated in everything that went on at the church. He baptized about 12-15 of the Sudduth and Wilson children. He baptized my sisters and cousins and me at the same time. Life at Zion was a beautiful experience and I'll never forget my wonderful upbringing.

Ms. Paulette Sudduth

Acknowledgments

I thank God, he is in the blessing business and used my grandfather's life as an example of how to live life victoriously. I pray that people will embrace the idea that we are here on earth to care for one another. I thank God for giving me the strength and the fortitude to write this book and I pray that it will be a blessing to the people it reaches.

I want to thank my husband Rev. Gerald Garth for his unwavering love and support during the creation of the book. I want to acknowledge all my friends and family who continually encouraged me to complete the book. I also want to acknowledge the kind words of the people who wrote comments about the personal memories of my grandfather and his relationships to the people, church and the community.

I want to give special thanks to Ms. Alysia Dunlap who helped who transform my writing into a living breathing story, Ms. Donna Kay Harris and Ms. Sheryl Murray who used their expertise to make the words singing in harmony. I am eternally grateful that I had the opportunity to work with these outstanding ladies who were instrumental in helping me complete phase I of my family legacy project.

Printed in the United States
By Bookmasters